EXTREME MONEY
HOW TO CONQUER PERSONAL FINANCE

DAN GASAPO

Copyright © 2018 Dan Gasapo
All rights reserved.

ISBN: 198770388X
ISBN-13: 978-1987703887

DEDICATION

To all the coaches, teachers, and mentors I have had the privilege of learning from. Each has had a unique impact on my life, and I am grateful for them all.

Preface

I write this book for the person who has never learned about personal finance or could use help understanding it better. Every day financial decisions are made affecting people's lives for better or worse. My goal is to explain to you the importance of personal finance and to educate you on how the tools work, so that you can monitor and improve your financial position. Knowing that my true calling is teaching and coaching, I have a passion to spread this knowledge with patience, simplicity, and as much excitement as possible so that you can understand how money works and become more confident in your personal finances.

Four and a half years ago I left my hometown to carve my own path and settled in a city 1,700 miles away with the goal of finding stable work and having fun. Shortly into my adventure I found work at one of the best-managed banks as a credit analyst. My first order of duty was learning credit, which is how banks make loans to businesses by underwriting the merits of the borrower and mitigating any risks. Credit is truly only learned through experience.

To jumpstart my learning process the bank sent me to credit training, where terminology, cash flow analysis, and loan structuring were discussed ad nauseam. After graduating credit training, I was anxious to get back into the office and start contributing to the team. Little did I know my training had actually just begun. The practice loans I underwrote in training were down the middle fairway credits, whereas the real-life loans I was tasked with always had a knot or two that tripped me up. My senior bosses relentlessly pointed out issues I had missed, which now I am grateful for. After multiple embarrassments I began asking questions beforehand to get in front of issues I hadn't experienced yet. Day after day and new loan after new loan I slowly built up knowledge and experience. Two years later suddenly everything clicked, and I began running through loans easier and more confidently.

The material I learned is nothing short of monumental, especially today where money, like it or not has a bearing in almost every decision we make. Knowing how financial statements work, the implications of debt, what interest rates signify, the importance of liquidity, and why compound interest is so valuable are the lynchpins of a financially-informed life. Knowing just these topics will propel you to succeed in achieving your personal finance goals.

It is unfortunate that this material being extremely relevant is rarely, if ever taught in high schools or colleges. Even I, who received a finance degree didn't understand the details of student debt or mechanics of a balance sheet until I was fully immersed in it every day. And that is why I am writing this book, because after school we are thrown into the workforce without any clue about financial matters critical to our livelihood.

I encourage you to take your time with this book and personal finance in general. The subject cannot be learned overnight. Only with consistent effort and a willingness to learn new topics will you make significant strides in conquering personal finance. I hope you enjoy this book and that it pays massive dividends for your future!

Contents

ESSENTIAL TOOLS
1. Balance Sheet — 9
2. Income Statement — 13

USING THE TOOLS
3. Budgeting — 17
4. Student Debt — 22
5. Saving — 26

INVESTING
6. Compound Interest — 27
7. Investments, Diversification, and Risk — 29
8. Retirement Accounts — 35

EVERYDAY FINANCE
9. Interest Rates — 38
10. Credit Score — 42
11. Banks v. Credit Unions v. Brokerage Firms — 45
12. Credit and Debit Cards — 47
13. Insurance — 50

ENTREPRENEURSHIP & BANKING
14. Loans and How They are Approved — 52
15. Developing a Business Plan — 56

MAJOR PURCHASES
16. Buying a Vehicle — 58
17. Buying a House — 61

MINDSET
18. Wealth — 67
19. Becoming Rich — 68
20. Until Next Time… — 71

Chapter 1: Balance Sheet

Assets			Liabilities	
Cash on Hand	100		Taxes Owing	-
Checking Account	1,000		Rent Due	500
Savings Account	3,000		Credit Card Debt	500
Health Savings Account	400		**Current Liabilities**	**1,000**
Marketable Securities	2,000			
Total Liquidity	**6,500**		Student Loan	10,000
			Auto Loan	6,000
Notes and Accounts Receivable	-		Mortgage Note	-
Real Estate - House	-		Other Liabilities	-
Real Estate - Other	-		**Total Liabilities**	**17,000**
IRA and 401(k) Accounts	15,500			
Personal Property & Automobiles	10,000		**NET WORTH**	**15,000**
Total Assets	**32,000**		**Total Liabilities & Net Worth**	**32,000**

Assets – Liabilities = Net Worth

A balance sheet is a financial statement that reflects your net worth at a specific point in time. It is used by businesses as well as individuals and is the basic tool to track your financial position.

I first understood the significance of a balance sheet after I started working at the bank, and realizing I had a sizeable amount of student debt. Knowing I had this liability frustrated me yet motivated me to pay it off faster. Without knowing how a balance sheet works, I may still be paying off my student loans today.

The three components to the balance sheet are assets, liabilities, and worth.

Assets are resources with monetary value such as cash, bank deposits, stocks, bonds, 401K and IRA accounts, real estate, automobiles, note receivables, and other personal property.

It is important to differentiate liquid and non-liquid assets. The economic term liquidity means how quickly can an asset be turned into cash. Hence, cash is the most liquid asset. Marketable securities like stocks and bonds can be sold much quicker and at market prices compared to selling your house. It may take months to sell your house at the market price, because you need a real-estate agent to market the house and find a buyer willing to pay the price you want for it. Therefore, stocks and bonds traded in a brokerage account are much more liquid than real estate.

Liabilities
Economic obligations that you must pay for now or in the future. For an individual, these include credit card debt, auto loan, and mortgage or rent payment. Any other financed items, or future obligations are also included.

Debt
Sometimes we think that having debt is bad, but liabilities like car loans, mortgages, and loans for education help people have things they want now but cannot afford to pay for up-front. It is practical to use debt to buy a house, car, or pay for education, because then you can use the good or service while paying for it overtime.

The trick about debt is to use it correctly and not to have too much of it. Used correctly, loans can significantly advance one's wealth. The right amount is dependent upon what you can sustainably afford throughout your expected future. Debt causes trouble when too much of it is taken on, and you are unable to satisfy the payments.

Net Worth
Simply your assets minus your liabilities. For example, if you have assets of $75,000 and liabilities of $20,000, then your net worth is $55,000.

Note – Since many merchants offer financing on big-ticket items, it is not uncommon for individuals to have monthly payments on their furniture, electronics, refrigerator, or other appliances. I recommend against financing these items, because it is best to have sufficient savings to cover these purchases. However, if you are in this position and need to finance a durable good, then practically speaking it is better to downsize and get the full mattress instead of the king, or the 36-inch TV instead of the 72-inch TV. The reason is, you already lack sufficient savings to cover the purchase, therefore by minimizing the total amount of debt you assume, you'll be able to pay off the loan faster, and start saving sooner.

It is acceptable to make large purchases with a credit card but understand that you should have the cash to pay the credit card bill in full. The only time I recommend financing appliances or items through the store is if the store gives you zero interest with no hidden fees and gives you the same price as if you were going to pay with cash or card.

Below is an example of an acceptable and a sub-standard personal balance sheet with explanations of why and general recommendations.

Acceptable Balance Sheet

Assets		Liabilities	
Cash on Hand	100	Taxes Owing	-
Checking Account	1,000	Rent Due	600
Savings Account	3,000	Credit Card Debt	400
Health Savings Account	400	**Current Liabilities**	**1,000**
Marketable Securities	-		
Total Liquidity	**4,500**	Student Loan	12,000
		Auto Loan	6,000
Notes and Accounts Receivable	-	Mortgage Note	-
Real Estate - House	-	Other Liabilities	-
Real Estate - Other	-	**Total Liabilities**	**19,000**
IRA and 401(k) Accounts	8,500		
Personal Property & Automobiles	10,000	**NET WORTH**	**4,000**
Total Assets	**23,000**	**Total Liabilities & Net Worth**	**23,000**

- Positive Net Worth
- Good Liquidity – $4,100 of liquid cash which is much greater than the $1,000 of current liabilities. Note that monthly payments for student debt, auto loan, and any other recurring obligations are considered a current liability.
- Acceptable Emergency Savings of $3,000.
- Investments – Even though the individual has debt, it is wise to begin investing versus plowing all excess cash flow into debt repayment.

I recommend continue contributing to your 401k or IRA to take advantage of compound interest while also paying down debt. Excess cash flow after 401k or IRA contributions should be used to first pay off student loan debt first, and then auto debt.

Substandard Balance Sheet

Assets		Liabilities	
Cash on Hand	100	Taxes Owing	-
Checking Account	1,000	Rent Due	500
Savings Account	-	Credit Card Debt	3,000
Health Savings Account	-	**Current Liabilities**	**3,500**
Marketable Securities	-		
Total Liquidity	**1,100**	Student Loan	-
		Auto Loan	6,000
Notes and Accounts Receivable	-	Mortgage Note	-
Real Estate - House	-	Other Liabilities	-
Real Estate - Other	-	**Total Liabilities**	**9,500**
IRA and 401(k) Accounts	-		
Personal Property & Automobiles	10,000	**NET WORTH**	**1,600**
Total Assets	**11,100**	**Total Liabilities & Net Worth**	**11,100**

- Insufficient Liquidity – Only $1,100 of cash to cover $3,500 of current liabilities.
- No savings and no investments.

I recommend reducing credit card debt by focusing only on the necessities and start a budgeting plan so as not to get into credit card debt again. Once you have developed a budget and paid down credit card debt, I recommend opening both a savings account and a retirement account. Begin contributing to both with the goal of building up a savings account of 3-9 months of expenses while consistently adding to an investment account. Remember, it may take a couple years to build that emergency savings account so be patient. Consistency and discipline will pay off.

Download Balance Sheet Template from:
https://goo.gl/BBVzbo

The link will send you to Extreme Money's Google Docs website where you can view and download templates for your own use. I highly recommend tracking your finances in spreadsheets like Google Docs or Microsoft Excel, or even writing it out by hand. Use whatever method works best for you.

Chapter 2: Income Statement

Personal Income Statement		
For One Month		
Income:	$	%
Work Income (after tax & 401k)	2,500	100%
Other/Misc. income	-	0%
Total Income	**2,500**	**100%**
Expense:		
Rent/Mortgage	500	20%
Student Debt	400	16%
Auto Loan	300	12%
Entertainment	200	8%
Groceries	150	6%
Dining Out	150	6%
Utilties	75	3%
Phone	75	3%
Personal/Burden	70	3%
Insurance	65	3%
Gasoline	60	2%
Clothes	50	2%
Gym	50	2%
Charity	25	1%
Total Cash Out	**2,170**	**87%**
CASH FLOW SURPLUS (Deficit)	**330**	**13%**

The income statement is a vital financial tool that reflects how much income you have left after accounting for all your expenses during a specified period of time. It monitors your income and spending. The income statement can be daily, weekly, monthly, or yearly.

Story - I did not grasp the importance of the income statement until I ran out of money even though I was making more money than I ever had been before! How was this happening I wondered? Instantly, I took the tools I learned from the bank and implemented them into my personal life. I began tracking how much I made each week, and how much I spent each week. I tracked every dollar I spent and did this on a weekly basis to find out where the money was going. Quickly, I realized I was literally throwing money away during the weekends by spending with reckless abandon on entertainment, restaurants, taxis, and clothes I did not need. Although feeling foolish, over the next few weeks I made small changes to my spending behavior, which resulted in more money leftover in my bank account. The ability to track income and expenses makes the income statement paramount for achieving financial success.

Components
For businesses, there is top-line revenue, which is what the company collects when it sells its product or service. Below that is typically the largest expense which is cost of goods sold. This is the cost of raw materials, and other production costs. Further below that is overhead, which is rent expense, utility expense, and other expenses to maintain the building. The remaining expenses are employee benefits, insurance, and other general and administrative costs. Taking the difference of revenue and the aforementioned expenses yields pre-tax profit, which is the bottom-line of the income statement. Lastly, the final expense is taxes. Everyone and every business must pay them.

For individuals it is the same concept, but personally tailored for you. Instead of revenue on the top, use net pay, which is after-taxes and 401k contributions, if your employer offers one. This makes it easier because now all you are accounting for is the net pay that is actually disbursed into your bank account. For salaried workers this is usually a fixed amount every two-weeks. Others who work variable hours or receive commissions or sales bonuses will have more income fluctuation. It is just as important to account for income fluctuations as it is for expenses, because knowing when and why your income changes will allow you to better plan for the future. Plus, knowing why may provide insights into how to make more!

Analyzing a Personal Income Statement

Personal Income Statement		
For One Month		
Income:	$	%
Work Income (after tax & 401k)	2,500	100%
Other/Misc. income	-	0%
Total Income	2,500	100%
Expense:		
Rent/Mortgage	500	20%
Student Debt	400	16%
Auto Loan	300	12%
Entertainment	200	8%
Groceries	150	6%
Dining Out	150	6%
Utilties	75	3%
Phone	75	3%
Personal/Burden	70	3%
Insurance	65	3%
Gasoline	60	2%
Clothes	50	2%
Gym	50	2%
Charity	25	1%
Total Cash Out	2,170	87%
CASH FLOW SURPLUS (Deficit)	330	13%

For simplicity purposes, lets analyze a hypothetical income statement. First, find out what your monthly income after-tax and 401k contributions is. Second, add-up all your expenses for the month, and group them into specific expense accounts like pictured above (rent, student debt, groceries, etc.) Organize the expense groups from highest to lowest. Typically rent or mortgage is the most, then student debt payment, car payment, utilities (water, energy, electricity, cable), cell-phone, groceries, insurance, medical payments, gym membership, entertainment, restaurants, trips, personal items, clothes, and charity. Unless you have kids, most of your expenses should fit in the line-items above.

It is helpful to common-size your income statement, which means showing every expense account as a percentage of income. This allows you to see what percent of your money is going where. For example, if rent is $500 and your monthly income is $2,500, then rent comprises 20% of your income. Common-sizing your income statement allows you to see trends, surprises, and make plans. For example, if you buy the same amount of groceries each month and on average it costs $150, then it's easy to assume you'll spend about $150 on groceries next month amounting to 6 percent of your income. This is a consistent, near fixed expense. On the other hand, a surprise or non-recurring expense would be taking a spur-of-the-moment trip to visit friends. Airfare, restaurant bills, entertainment expenses, and ATM withdrawals total $500. This amounts to 20 percent of monthly income and took place over just a couple days. Occasionally this is fine but be cognizant not to make this a habit or else you will soon run out of money.

Cash Flow Surplus (Deficit)

After subtracting all expenses from income, you will come up with your cash flow surplus or deficit. This amount should be used to build up savings or to make additional debt repayments.

Cash flow deficits result from spending more money than you made. This means you either borrowed on credit or dipped into your savings to pay for your expenses. A deficit is understandable occasionally especially when you make large purchases, however having regular deficits is a sign of poor financial management and will lead to economic hardship.

Download Income Statement Template from:
https://goo.gl/BBVzbo

Chapter 3: Budgeting

The people who budget are confident about their financial position because they know where they are and what their plan is.

What Is the Goal of Budgeting?
1. Get you to where you want to be financially
2. Become more confident about your financial position

Without a budget how do you expect to meet your financial goals? How do you know where you financially stand? Most people do not budget nor track their expenses. They make financial decisions solely based on the amount of cash in their bank account. This is akin to a coach showing up to a game with no game plan, calling plays on intuition only, and wondering why his team consistently underperforms. Unfortunately, this coach fails to succeed because he fails to prepare. If this is like your current financial state, do not get down on yourself, because starting with only a few small changes today can substantially improve your finances in the future. Below is a simple budgeting method consisting of the two tools you just learned about: the balance sheet and income statement.

People have all sorts of different financial goals, but for many they boil down to reducing debt or saving more.

1. Find Out Where You Stand
Budgeting starts with knowing your current financial position, also known as your assets, liabilities, and net worth. See Chapter 1 to create your own balance sheet. Complete this is in a spreadsheet or notebook to track progress.

Assets		Liabilities	
Cash on Hand	-	Taxes Owing	-
Checking Account	4,000	Rent Due	500
Savings Account	-	Credit Card Debt	300
Health Savings Account	500	**Current Liabilities**	**800**
Marketable Securities	-		
Total Liquidity	**4,500**	Student Loan	-
		Auto Loan	4,200
Notes and Accounts Receivable	-	Mortgage Note	-
Real Estate - House	-	Other Liabilities	-
Real Estate - Other	-	**Total Liabilities**	**5,000**
IRA and 401(k) Accounts	3,500		
Personal Property & Automobiles	10,000	**NET WORTH**	**13,000**
Total Assets	**18,000**	**Total Liabilities & Net Worth**	**18,000**

2. **Track Your Past Expenses**
   a. Fill out your income statement over the last month. **Include all income and every expense.** Round to the nearest dollar for simplicity.
   b. Group expenses by category using the income statement below.
   c. Common-size all expense groups (expressing expenses as a percentage of net income).
   d. Complete your income statement ending with Cash Flow Surplus/Deficit.

"Beware of little expenses; a small leak will sink a great ship."
- Benjamin Franklin

Personal Income Statement For One Month		
Income:	**$**	**%**
Work Income (after tax & 401k)	2,100	100%
Other/Misc. income	-	0%
Total Income	**2,100**	**100%**
Expense:		
Rent/Mortgage	500	24%
Student Debt	300	14%
Auto Loan	250	12%
Entertainment	200	10%
Dining Out	150	7%
Groceries	150	7%
Utilties	75	4%
Phone	60	3%
Insurance	60	3%
Gym	50	2%
Gasoline	40	2%
Personal/Burden	25	1%
Charity	20	1%
Clothes	-	0%
Car Maintenance	-	0%
Total Cash Out	**1,880**	**90%**
CASH FLOW SURPLUS (Deficit)	**220**	**10%**

3. **Review and Analyze**
   a. Analyze your past month's income statement and highlight anything that sticks out to you.
   b. Are you concerned with how much money goes to certain places? People frequently spend too much on rent, entertainment, restaurants, auto payments, and excessive non-essential items like clothing or home furnishings.

Reflect
Take a minute to reflect on each expense that stands out. Think about whether that expense was worth it. Knowing what you know now, would you still have made that same purchase? If not, then you would have that money left over for more productive uses like reducing debt, increasing savings, or investing, all which improve your financial position.

After reflecting on your last month's income statement, if you have a fixed salary, and you spend the same amount next month, then you will know exactly what your cash flow surplus or deficit will be. However, if you make a couple adjustments by cutting out a few nonessential expenses then you will have that additional amount of money left over to further increase savings or reduce debt, or to buy something you really want but thought you could never afford.

Setting a Budget
1. Next to each variable expense group, set a realistic number you want to stick to. For example, if you spent $250 at restaurants last month, but know you can have similar enjoyment spending only $125, set your restaurant budget at $125.
    - Be realistic about your budget. If you have student debt that you want paid down quickly, then allowing yourself a monthly restaurant budget of $400 is not practical and certainly not conducive to your goals. It would be wiser to cook your meals at home, which is cheaper, thereby freeing up more money to reduce student debt. Do this for every expense group.

2. Fixed expenses like rent, cell-phone, car payment, and insurance cannot be changed until you either move-out, request a change, refinance, or solicit a second opinion and change carriers.
    - Reducing your rent, but still enjoying where you live is the most effective way to maximize cash flow with little effort. It is a trade-off, but moving into an apartment that is $200 cheaper saves you $2,400 over the year.
    - To get the most out of budgeting, you must reduce spending on expense groups that make a meaningful difference. If bringing your lunch to work instead of going to restaurants saves $10 a day, that would increase cash flow by about $215 more per month, or $2,580 per year. That's a good chunk of money that can be used to get closer to your goals.

3. For the next month think about each purchase you make and how it relates to your budget. After the month ends, complete your income statement, and evaluate your performance.
    - Where did you succeed?
    - Where did you fail?
    - Are you surprised with how you did?
    - What can you improve on?
    - Were any of your budget targets unrealistic? If so, appropriately change them to reflect your goals.

Budgeting is about goals.
Achieving those goals requires sacrifice and discipline.

If you want to pay-off debt as soon as possible, prepare yourself to forego expensive dinners, fancy new clothes, and any other nonessential splurges. The same principle applies when saving for your first emergency fund, big trip, down payment for a house, or any other large expenditure.

Sacrifice + Commitment = Success

Managing Surprise Expenses
It can be hard to feel in control of your finances when surprise expenses arise. For example, you have worked hard at building an emergency savings account and suddenly your vehicle needs repair and the cost will wipe out half of it. Although demoralizing, you have actually succeeded, because you will not be going into debt to pay for this repair. Furthermore, you have experienced the importance of having this savings and know you are capable of building it back up again. When setbacks like this occur, stay optimistic and know that there will be more days ahead to work and grow your savings.

Vacation, Bachelor, & Bachelorette Parties
Oftentimes our financial goals come into conflict with life. Opportunities arise that we know will cost money. These may include weddings, bachelor parties, vacation, or spontaneous trips. Invitations come, and plans are made, but what about the cost? It is difficult to tell your friends no to a party on account of cost, however this is a real issue for our generation. Use the tips below when life conflicts with your financial goals.
- Communicate with your friends and family.
- Recognize the importance of events like a best-friend's wedding, a major family vacation, or even a funeral
- Gauge your future earnings. Maybe you can swing the flight and other expenses knowing you will pare back expenses afterward.

Events like these are the reason why you save. Whether it's car repairs, medical bills, bachelor parties, or what have you, start saving now to cover these future events. Life happens, be prepared for it.

Say No
Sometimes you may just need to say no! How will you ever get ahold of your money if you only say yes to every opportunity that comes your way? This includes everything: going out to restaurants or bars, spontaneous trips, donation requests, and much more. Take ownership of your finances by making decisions that will help you.

Chapter 4: Student Debt

Story – During high school I never seriously thought about college. I was too busy enjoying the freedom of having a car, partying with my friends, and mowing lawns and working part-time jobs that put cash in my pocket. Yet, I always knew I would go to college, because that was what everyone else was doing, and was constantly preached as the right thing to do by my teachers and parents. For me, there was no alternative. It was either go to college or move out and find work on my own. I ended up enrolling at the local community college, because frankly I didn't exert much effort into the application process. At the time, the whole thing seemed silly to me. Studying test material that made little sense, and staring at the overwhelmingly amount of required forms just to apply quickly damped my desire to continue submitting applications. Upon reflection I was happy how it ended up because I didn't have to change much to go to community college, and it prepared me well for the transition from high school to college.

Although I was happy to graduate and proud of my hard work, I was befuddled that I owed a lot of money to some company called Great Lakes Higher Education Corporation. I knew that I would have student debt, but was unaware of how much, whom I owed it to, or anything about how the process worked. I just looked at that number, and thought, "Oh no!" Clearly, I had signed some forms to take this debt out, and now I was on the hook for paying it back.

The Light Bulb
After graduation I made the minimum payment for about the first 12 months while working odd jobs like valeting cars and bussing tables. During this time, I hadn't learned the mechanics of loans yet, and thought the minimum payment was sufficient. Then, I got the job at the bank and undertook credit training. There I became immersed in the fundamentals of debt, and how loans work. We analyzed pricing and loan payments through Microsoft Excel. The spreadsheet had two columns; one for principle and the other for interest. After entering in a loan amount, the term, and the interest rate, I visually saw how expensive loans could be. Suddenly, I thought about my own student debt and how much I was paying in interest.

Taking Action
Instantly I went home and logged into my Great Lakes account, and viewed my balances, terms, interest rates, and payments. I was shocked at

how much interest I was paying! By then I knew enough about debt that there was nothing I could do to change how much the principal was. But I knew I could do something about the interest I owed and vowed to pay as little as possible. From that day on it was like I found a new religion; eliminating student debt as fast as possible, and not to give Great Lakes any more money than I already owed them. I was on a mission.

Student Loan Components
Just to review: a loan is money lent to someone for something, to be repaid at a later day plus interest. There are four components of a loan:
- **Principal** – Amount borrowed
- **Loan Term** – Timeline for when loan is to be repaid usually expressed in months or years
- **Interest Rate** – The rate used to calculate the amount of interest expense borrower is required to pay lender
- **Payment** – The amount of principal and interest due each period determined by the principal, term, and interest rate. Generally, payments are required monthly

Student loan payments are calculated through an amortization schedule. Amortization means the borrower will pay a fixed amount each month, which includes both principal and interest. Fixed rate mortgages and auto loans are also calculated this way.

Example
After graduation, a student has $35,000 in total student debt (principal) and signs up for a 120 month (10 year) repayment plan with an annual interest rate of 6.00%. The monthly payment is $388.57, which includes both principal and interest.

Annual Breakdown of P&I Payments

Year	Interest	Principal	Total % of Principal
1	$ 2,028	$ 2,635	7.5%
2	$ 1,866	$ 2,797	8.0%
3	$ 1,693	$ 2,970	8.5%
4	$ 1,510	$ 3,153	9.0%
5	$ 1,316	$ 3,347	9.6%
6	$ 1,109	$ 3,554	10.2%
7	$ 890	$ 3,773	10.8%
8	$ 657	$ 4,005	11.4%
9	$ 410	$ 4,253	12.2%
10	$ 148	$ 4,515	12.9%
Total	$11,629	$35,000	100%

Notes
1. Assuming the borrower only made the minimum payment throughout the life of the loan, interest expense would be $11,629. That would make the total cost of the student loan to be $46,629, of which interest expense makes up 25%. This amount is much more than borrowers initially realize, which makes it critically important to see how additional principal payments can reduce this number in the next example.
2. Due to the amortization schedule, interest expense is paid in the earlier stages of the loan term. The arrow to the right of the chart shows principal payments getting larger as the loan nears maturity, which is the opposite for interest expense. The monthly payment stays the same. It is just the proportion of principal and interest that changes throughout the loan term.

Same Example with Additional Principal Payment
Keeping everything the same in the prior example, except instead of making the minimum monthly payment of $388.57, the borrower pays $300 more in principal payments for a total payment of $688.57. **Notice the difference in interest.**

Annual Breakdown of P&I Payments

Year	Interest	Principal	Total % of Principal
1	$ 1,928	$ 6,335	18.1%
2	$ 1,537	$ 6,726	19.2%
3	$ 1,122	$ 7,141	20.4%
4	$ 682	$ 7,581	21.7%
5	$ 215	$ 7,217	20.6%
Total	$ 5,483	$35,000	100%

Notes
1. The borrower pays the loan off in half the time.
2. The borrower saved $6,145 in total interest expense, making the total cost of debt $40,483. Interest expense only accounts for 13.5% in this example, compared to the 25% in the prior example.

Summary
It is unfortunate that higher education costs have risen at mind-boggling rates over the last two decades and students are the ones to bear the brunt of it. There are many reasons for this but primarily it is due to less

government funding, easier access to student loans, and a case of supply and demand. First, higher education is competitive, and schools have had to raise tuition to offer more programs and services that attract prospective students. Second, the government and other lenders are willing to finance these higher costs. Third, federal and state budgets have reduced funding to higher education to pay for entitlement programs which continually take up a larger share of government spending.

Society is beginning to recognize the social costs student debt has on people and debating whether college is even worth it. I firmly believe in the importance of education; however, students today need to understand the implications of the debt they assume and weigh the benefits with the costs.

However unfair or bad the system may be, this is the reality we live in. No matter how much we complain, borrowers are still on the hook to pay back their student loans. That said, mentally prepare yourself to pay this debt off. Whether it takes five years or twenty years, visualize the day you make that last payment, and the joy of relief knowing you are free from student debt.

Chapter 5: Saving

The ones who save rest easy at night, knowing they are prepared for the unexpected. People complicate saving and make excuses for why they cannot save, but budgeting should only take an hour or so each week to prepare, plan, and analyze. The hard part is simply commitment.

Reasons to Save

Emergencies – Having an emergency fund gives you options for unexpected expenses. You avoid having to go into debt to pay for repairs, surgery, or other unforeseen events. Rule of thumb is 3-9 months of expenses. Amount depends on your situation: single, married, dependents, and job reliability.

Peace of Mind – Having extra cash in the bank significantly reduces financial anxiety, because you know you have a cushion in the event of being laid off or if you need the money for a big trip.

Earn a Return on Your Money – Savings can be used for investments. Once you meet your emergency savings need you can deploy excess savings to earn a higher rate of return compared to a savings account.

Down Payment on a House – Buying a house is the American Dream. Having a sufficient down payment makes the process easier.

Options – If you have built up sufficient savings, and confident about your financial position, then you are free to do what you want.

Story – Mike had a regular job where he worked at for three years. During those years, he practiced sound budgeting and built up sufficient emergency savings in addition to his retirement savings. He also sacrificed and paid off his remaining student debt. Mike still had fun when he was working, and probably could have saved more, but he was diligent about monitoring his budget. After some soul-searching Mike came to grips that his work was not rewarding to him but didn't know what to do. He just knew he didn't like what he was doing. So, feeling confident in his financial position, Mike resigned, consolidated his things, and took off for a couple trips. He did things he always wanted to do like travel, volunteer, and see family. Mike did all these things without having a job lined up, because he was confident about his financial position knowing how long his savings would last him. Mike was only able to accomplish this because he was committed to and practiced sound budgeting.

Chapter 6: Compound Interest

Albert Einstein once said, *"Compound interest is the eighth wonder of the world. He who understands it, earns it... he who doesn't... pays it."* This quote, from perhaps the most well-known scientist epitomizes the sheer magnitude and value of compound interest. Lucky for you, by investing sooner rather than later, you can capture the benefit of compound interest, and reap its reward as you grow older and near retirement.

Compound interest is primarily related to investing. Its definition is the addition of interest earned to the original principal, thereby making the principal larger for the next interest payments. Basically, it's the interest earned on the interest. Investors earn interest from share price appreciation and dividends. The investor will be rewarded with compound interest by holding onto the investment and reinvesting the dividends, making the investment principal larger. Since the principal balance is now larger, future share price appreciation and dividends will also be larger, ultimately compounding your total investment. See the chart below to see how it works.

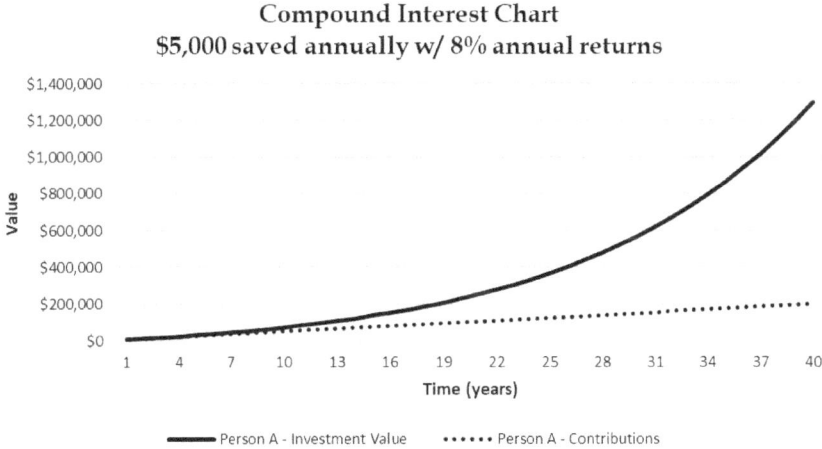

Look at the chart above. The dotted line reflects the total amount of contributions invested, while the solid line reflects the total value of your investment. See the difference! After 40 years, one invested only $200,000 yet the investment is worth over $1.2 million. That is the magic of compound interest.

Time Is the Most Important Factor

Starting early is extremely beneficial, because it allows investors to capture more value of compound interest. See the chart below, which illustrates how dramatic a difference time plays in the value compound interest has on your investment account.

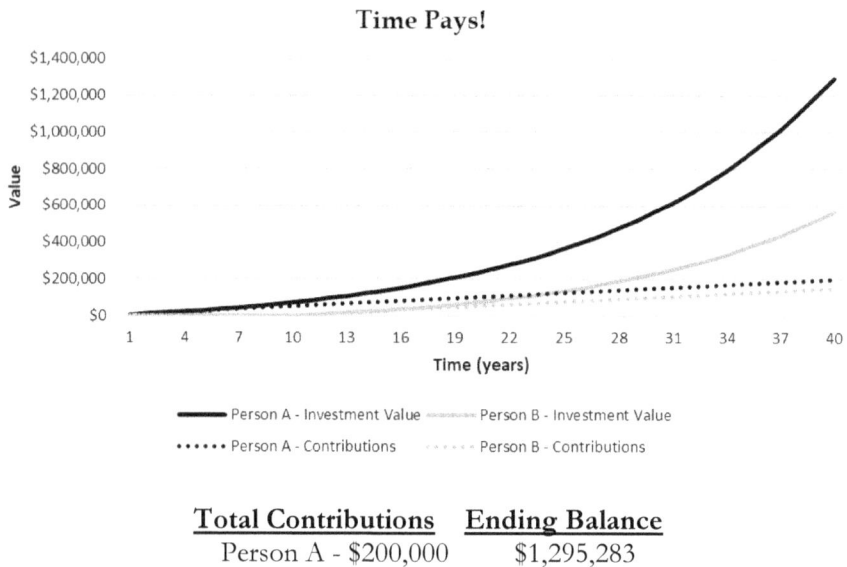

Total Contributions	Ending Balance
Person A - $200,000	$1,295,283
Person B - $150,000	$566,416

Both Person A and Person B contribute $5,000 a year into their investment account. Each receive 8% annual returns. Person A starts 10 years earlier than Person B. Although Person A invested $50,000 more than Person B, she ended up with a balance of $728,867 greater than Person B, because she benefited from the 10 additional years of compounding interest. Talk about a monumental difference!

Chapter 7: Investments, Diversification, and Risk

People invest to earn a return on their money. Investors come in all shapes and sizes, and with a 401k or an Investment Retirement Account you yourself are also an investor. It does not matter how much you have. If you are contributing to your 401k or buying stocks you are deploying money to earn a return, thus making you an investor.

There is an awful stigma in America, where people think that if they have little money, they should not or cannot invest. This is the complete opposite of what you should be doing. Starting off small is the best way to begin, because it is much easier and tolerable to learn from your mistakes when your portfolio is just beginning as compared to when you are nearing retirement in which mistakes can be far costlier. Plus, with today's technology, investment and brokerage companies offer a plethora of advice and make it simple to open an account and begin investing.

Since most employers no longer offer pensions it becomes your responsibility to save for retirement. And don't count on social security for a stable income, because the program is not expected to provide comfortable benefits in the future.

Risk – The possibility that you will lose your entire investment, and the chance your actual return will not be what you expected.

Return – The gain or loss on an investment over a period of time. For example, if you purchase one share of Apple stock at $100, and after one year, the stock price is $120. Your annual return is 20%.

The Risk/Reward chart on the prior page illustrates that higher risk investments have higher expected returns. Startups have the highest risk of failure, yet the ones that succeed yield enormous returns on their investment. A certificate of deposit, which is near risk-free has a much smaller return compared to stocks or real estate. Investments with higher degrees of risk command higher degrees of return.

Common Investments
- **Stocks** – Also called equities. Stocks are an ownership share of a publicly traded company. Stockholders have equity in the company and are entitled to a portion of the company's income through dividends or buybacks. The stock price is determined by market value, which is the highest price someone is willing to pay and the lowest price someone is willing to sell at.
- **Bonds** – Also called fixed income. Bonds are loans to companies and governments, where the borrower pays interest at regular intervals and pays the full principal back to the bondholder (investor) at loan maturity. Treasuries are loans to the U.S. government and are at fixed rates. Corporate bonds are loans to businesses and can be fixed or variable rate. Bondholders have no equity in the company, therefore receiving no dividends, however if the company fails, they normally have first dibs on its assets.
- **Certificate of Deposit** – A certificate issued by a bank to a person depositing money for a specific length of time. CD terms vary from 1 month to several years. The longer the term, the higher the interest rate. Withdrawing the money prior to maturity will incur penalties. The Federal Deposit Insurance Corporation (FDIC) insures CDs, checking, and savings accounts up to $250,000 making them near risk free.
- **Exchange Traded Fund (ETF)** – Ownership share in a fund that invests in certain indices and trades like a stock. ETFs can be a collection of stocks or bonds and have become popular because the majority track a certain index giving them broad diversification and have lower expense ratios than mutual funds.
- **Mutual Fund** – An investment fund that is professionally managed and is usually diversified. Mutual funds are actively managed, where a manager buys and sells investments at will in accordance with the fund's guidelines. This contrasts with ETFs, which are passively managed and only track a certain index.
- **Real Estate** – Owning a rental property increases diversification, because it broadens your portfolio beyond the traditional stock and bond allocation. Although acceptable, a strict stock and bond portfolio no matter how diversified suffers from systemic risk of

market failure since all are traded on markets. However, a rental property is immune from this non-diversifiable risk as it is not traded on an exchange and the source of income is from a tenant who you can physically contact to collect the rental payment.

- **Real Estate Investment Trust (REIT)** – You can invest in real estate through your retirement or brokerage account by owning a REIT. These are companies that own or finance rental real estate including student housing, single-family homes, multi-family apartments, and commercial office space. REITs pay out much of their income to shareholders in the form of dividends. REITs offer flexibility to investors because they trade like a stock and provide real estate exposure without having to physically own and manage a property.
- **Target Date Funds** – Provide a simple investment solution (one-fund only) whose portfolio asset allocation becomes more conservative as the target date (retirement) approaches. This allows investors to choose only one fund for their retirement account. Target date funds begin with higher risk assets and overtime the fund reduces risk as the target date approaches, thereby protecting your investment.
- **Index** – Not an investment, but often used as a benchmark for ETFs and Mutual Funds. Indices are a measurement of a collection of stocks or bonds. For example, the S&P 500 is an index that tracks the aggregate stock performance of the 500 largest publicly traded companies in the United States and is commonly looked at to describe how the overall U.S. market is performing.

Key Points to Investing
Time Horizon – When are you expecting to need the money? Time horizon dictates risk tolerance.
- If you need the money next month, it would be best to keep it in a savings or checking account because it is FDIC insured.
- If you don't need it until retirement, which is 40 years away, then you should diversify much or all of it into equities, because over time your return through appreciation and dividends will significantly outweigh negative swings in the market.

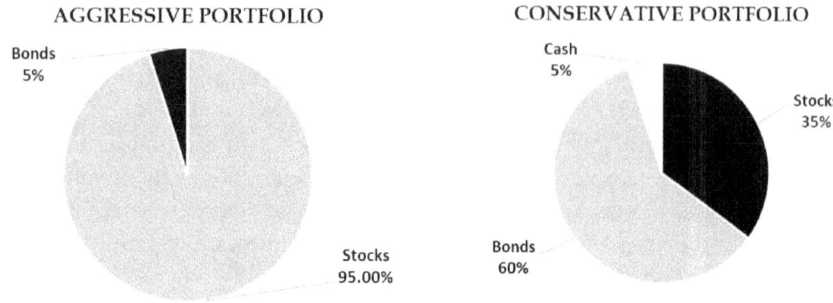

Risk Tolerance – How much risk are you willing to take? The more risk you take, the more you may earn, but you are also vulnerable to higher volatility and stock market crashes.
- If you are a millennial and saving for retirement, you should be invested in 70%-90% stocks through diversified ETFs or mutual funds. Since your time horizon is longer, you are better suited to weather major corrections in the market. This is compared to someone nearing retirement who should have a more conservative portfolio with 40%-70% invested in bonds due to their more stable returns yet lower appreciation.

Volatility – The variation of price changes for a stock, bond, or market index over a period of time and is measured from high to low.
- Markets and individual stocks exhibit high volatility when changes in price are dramatic and quick. Low volatility is when price changes are within smaller ranges and occur slower.
- This is important because volatility to the downside can scare investors into selling prematurely as they see their portfolio value suddenly decrease. This is the opposite of what long-term investors should do.
- Since market prices are dictated by information, prices can change very quickly as new information surfaces, both to the upside and downside. Be cautious not to overreact to information. Most of the time it is just market noise. If you are investing for the long-term be prepared to experience volatility. It is normal and an indication of well-functioning markets.

Diversification – Mixing your portfolio with various securities to not be significantly vulnerable to any one company. Diversifying your portfolio across different industries reduces the riskiness of the overall portfolio.

- If you are only invested in Company XYZ and suddenly XYZ announces it is negatively restating multiple prior years' earnings, the stock price may rapidly decrease, meaning your potential for losses is highly probable.
- Diversify through ETFs that track different segments of the stock market. For example, the S&P 500 tracks the performance of the 500 largest US stocks, and the Russell 3000 tracks the performance of the whole US stock market.

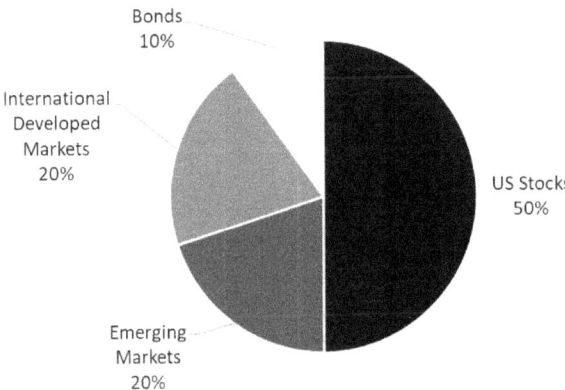

International and Emerging Markets
- Invest a portion in international developed markets like Europe or Australia, and emerging markets like China, South Korea, Taiwan, India, South Africa, Brazil and Mexico. Not only does this diversify your portfolio, it captures a share of the appreciation of these growing economies.
- Emerging markets often have higher growth rates than mature economies like the U.S. or Europe due to stronger demographics, decreased cost of labor, opening of trade, and access to foreign investment. However, it needs to be noted that emerging markets carry higher risk than mature markets due to political uncertainties, lax regulations and oversight, and currency fluctuations.

Capital (money) flows to the most productive assets. This means the companies and countries that are most efficient and effective at producing goods and services will see more capital allocated to it and overtime will generate stronger returns.

Stock v. Bonds Compounded Returns Over the Last 50 Years[1]

	Annual Returns on Investments in			Compounded Value of $ 100		
Year	S&P 500 (includes dividends)	3-month T.Bill	Return on 10-year T. Bond	Stocks	T.Bills	T.Bonds
1967	23.80%	4.33%	-1.58%	$ 124	$ 104	$ 98
1968	10.81%	5.26%	3.27%	$ 137	$ 110	$ 102
1969	-8.24%	6.56%	-5.01%	$ 126	$ 117	$ 97
1970	3.56%	6.69%	16.75%	$ 130	$ 125	$ 113
1971	14.22%	4.54%	9.79%	$ 149	$ 131	$ 124
1972	18.76%	3.95%	2.82%	$ 177	$ 136	$ 127
1973	-14.31%	6.73%	3.66%	$ 152	$ 145	$ 132
1974	-25.90%	7.78%	1.99%	$ 112	$ 156	$ 135
1975	37.00%	5.99%	3.61%	$ 154	$ 165	$ 139
1976	23.83%	4.97%	15.98%	$ 190	$ 174	$ 162
1977	-6.98%	5.13%	1.29%	$ 177	$ 183	$ 164
1978	6.51%	6.93%	-0.78%	$ 189	$ 195	$ 162
1979	18.52%	9.94%	0.67%	$ 224	$ 215	$ 164
1980	31.74%	11.22%	-2.99%	$ 295	$ 239	$ 159
1981	-4.70%	14.30%	8.20%	$ 281	$ 273	$ 172
1982	20.42%	11.01%	32.81%	$ 338	$ 303	$ 228
1983	22.34%	8.45%	3.20%	$ 414	$ 328	$ 235
1984	6.15%	9.61%	13.73%	$ 439	$ 360	$ 268
1985	31.24%	7.49%	25.71%	$ 576	$ 387	$ 336
1986	18.49%	6.04%	24.28%	$ 683	$ 410	$ 418
1987	5.81%	5.72%	-4.96%	$ 723	$ 434	$ 397
1988	16.54%	6.45%	8.22%	$ 842	$ 462	$ 430
1989	31.48%	8.11%	17.69%	$ 1,107	$ 499	$ 506
1990	-3.06%	7.55%	6.24%	$ 1,073	$ 537	$ 538
1991	30.23%	5.61%	15.00%	$ 1,398	$ 567	$ 618
1992	7.49%	3.41%	9.36%	$ 1,502	$ 586	$ 676
1993	9.97%	2.98%	14.21%	$ 1,652	$ 604	$ 772
1994	1.33%	3.99%	-8.04%	$ 1,674	$ 628	$ 710
1995	37.20%	5.52%	23.48%	$ 2,296	$ 662	$ 877
1996	22.68%	5.02%	1.43%	$ 2,817	$ 696	$ 890
1997	33.10%	5.05%	9.94%	$ 3,750	$ 731	$ 978
1998	28.34%	4.73%	14.92%	$ 4,813	$ 765	$1,124
1999	20.89%	4.51%	-8.25%	$ 5,818	$ 800	$1,031
2000	-9.03%	5.76%	16.66%	$ 5,292	$ 846	$1,203
2001	-11.85%	3.67%	5.57%	$ 4,665	$ 877	$1,270
2002	-21.97%	1.66%	15.12%	$ 3,640	$ 892	$1,462
2003	28.36%	1.03%	0.38%	$ 4,673	$ 901	$1,467
2004	10.74%	1.23%	4.49%	$ 5,175	$ 912	$1,533
2005	4.83%	3.01%	2.87%	$ 5,425	$ 939	$1,577
2006	15.61%	4.68%	1.96%	$ 6,272	$ 983	$1,608
2007	5.48%	4.64%	10.21%	$ 6,616	$1,029	$1,772
2008	-36.55%	1.59%	20.10%	$ 4,198	$1,045	$2,129
2009	25.94%	0.14%	-11.12%	$ 5,286	$1,047	$1,892
2010	14.82%	0.13%	8.46%	$ 6,070	$1,048	$2,052
2011	2.10%	0.03%	16.04%	$ 6,197	$1,048	$2,381
2012	15.89%	0.05%	2.97%	$ 7,182	$1,049	$2,452
2013	32.15%	0.07%	-9.10%	$ 9,490	$1,050	$2,229
2014	13.52%	0.05%	10.75%	$10,774	$1,050	$2,468
2015	1.38%	0.21%	1.28%	$10,923	$1,052	$2,500
2016	11.77%	0.51%	0.69%	$12,208	$1,058	$2,517
2017	21.64%	1.39%	2.80%	$14,851	$1,072	$2,588

Notice the difference in returns between stocks and treasuries. Although stocks have years with significant losses, overtime stocks compounded returns far exceed that of bonds. See ending value in 2017.

---

[1] Damodaran, Aswath. *Annual Returns on Stock, T.Bonds and T.Bills: 1928 - Current.* 5 Jan. 2018, pages.stern.nyu.edu/~adamodar/New_Home_Page/datafile/histretSP.html.

Chapter 8: Retirement Accounts

Since you cannot work forever nor live comfortably off social security, saving for retirement is therefore crucial and prudent. No matter what your income is, you should have the ability to set aside a portion toward retirement. It is only a matter of priorities, and regularly setting aside even a small amount now has enormous earning potential in the future. Think compound interest.

This chapter will provide a broad overview of the retirement system and the different features of typical accounts. Having a basic understanding of the retirement landscape and contributing to a retirement account will set you up for long term success. Not saving or contributing to a retirement account will certainly result in dire circumstances upon retirement assuming you are even capable of retiring.

What Is It and How Does It Work?
Retirement accounts are used to save for retirement. The accounts invest in stocks, bonds, and other securities that earn higher returns than a standard savings account. The accounts are set up strictly for retirement purposes, which is why early withdrawals are penalized with fees.

Retirement Accounts and Pensions:
- **401(k)** – A retirement plan set up by an employer that allows employees to contribute pre or post tax income into an investment account (defined contribution plan). The account is managed by a third-party investment company that provides different investment options, and the ability to track account performance. Oftentimes, employers will contribute or match a certain percentage of money into your investment account. This encourages employees to save more and provides another benefit to working at the company. Take full advantage of the company match because it is free money!
- **403(b)** – Same thing as a 401(k) but for public employees and workers at nonprofit organizations.
- **Investment Retirement Account (IRA)** – These accounts are set up by the individual and have no relation to an employer. The company you choose to open an IRA with will provide a platform to invest in publicly traded securities, mutual funds, and ETFs. Individuals can choose pre-tax or post-tax contributions just like a 401(k).
    - **Pre-Tax** – Contributions into pre-tax accounts are tax-deductible. Meaning when you file your taxes, all contributions into your pre-tax 401k or IRA will reduce your taxable income

for that year, ultimately reducing your current year's tax bill. However, withdrawals during retirement will be taxed at the tax bracket you are in.
- o **Post-Tax (Roth)** – Individuals using Roth accounts will pay taxes on their contributions now, but the withdrawals during retirement will be tax-free.

How to Choose – The rule of thumb is that if you believe you will be in a higher tax bracket at retirement then you should contribute into after-tax (Roth) accounts. This allows you to collect withdrawals tax-free at retirement by paying the tax on it now. Sophisticated investors analyze other factors, because there is a grey area to this rule.

PENALTY FEES and TAXES are assessed if you withdraw funds from your 401(k), 403(b), or IRA prior to age 59 ½. There are few exceptions, and I highly advise against early withdrawals unless you face financial hardship, disability, or medical debt.

- **Pensions** – Fixed amount of money contributed to you after retirement typically in perpetuity meaning one will receive a fixed amount monthly until they pass away (defined benefit plan). Fewer and fewer companies provide pensions, because of its high costs, uncertainty, and the overall shifting landscape of retirement benefits. Yet many public service employees like government officials, military members, teachers, police officers, firefighters, and others are still entitled to pensions after completing a certain number of years.
  - o Pensions are attractive because of the certainty it provides retired people. Knowing that you will receive a guaranteed fixed income monthly for perpetuity relieves much financial stress one may experience nearing retirement.
  - o Pension amounts are dictated by an agreed upon formula which include:
    - Years an employee works at the organization
    - Compensation at or near retirement
    - Age
  - o Pensions are managed by a third-party who are required to meet certain investment goals in order to meet pension obligations.
  - o Employees and employers collectively contribute to the pension plan to fund its operation.

Key Points
- If you are not in a pension plan, the burden of saving for retirement falls on you. Even if you are in a pension plan it is prudent to open an unrelated IRA to diversify your retirement sources.
- Don't try to time the market.
- Enroll in auto-contributions.
- Always reinvest your dividends to ensure long-term growth.
- Rollover your 401k if you change employers.
- Early withdrawals face steep penalty fees and taxes.
- Set up beneficiaries on all 401k, pension, IRA, checking & savings accounts. Therefore, if an accident were to happen, the transfer of assets will be much simpler.
- The hardest part to saving for retirement is simply starting.

Chapter 9: Interest Rates

The foundation of money and finance revolves around interest. Everyone who participates in the economy is affected by interest in some way whether that is through an auto loan, mortgage, or credit card. It is to your advantage to understand how interest works so you can minimize borrowing costs and therefore have more money to save or invest.

Interest is simply the cost of borrowing money over a specified period of time. It is expressed as a percentage and the amount varies depending on what is being financed and other variables. Interest rates apply to mortgages, car loans, student loans, credit cards, home-equity loans, and other types of borrowing activity.

For example, as of February 2018 the average interest rate for a 60-month auto loan is 4.21%. Therefore, on a $25,000 car purchase, borrowers will have a monthly payment of $463 and pay $2,767 in total interest over the life of the loan. The interest cost makes up 11% of the purchase price of the vehicle. If you found a lender who provided a rate of 3.21% which is a full percentage point below the average, your total interest expense would be $2,093, which is $674 cheaper. Essentially this is free money and could be in your bank account if you just took the time to shop around for rates.

How is the Rate Determined?
Many factors are taken into consideration when receiving an interest rate. For borrowers it primarily depends on what is being financed and their creditworthiness. The Federal Reserve and the overall health of the economy play a major role in establishing baseline interest rates lenders use to price their loans, however borrowers have no influence on these external factors. The factors borrowers can control are:

Factors
- **Term** – How long will the loan be. The longer the term, the higher the rate because lenders require a premium for assuming more risk. Longer loans are deemed riskier because there is more opportunity for a borrower to default. Additionally, lenders need to be compensated for the opportunity cost of not being able to loan that money out at higher rates in the future.
- **Collateral** – Something pledged as security for repayment of the loan to be forfeited if the borrower defaults. Examples include:
    - House - Mortgage
    - Vehicle - Auto Loan

- - - 1st or 2nd Lien on House - Home Equity Loan
    - Marketable Securities - Margin Loan
    - Heavy Equipment - Business Loan
  - **Credit Report** – A score that rates your credit history. The range is 300-850. A good score is 700 or higher.
  - **Capacity** – Ability to pay back the loan. Lenders will require tax returns and other financial statements proving you have sufficient income to pay your debts.
  - **Capital and Loan Amount** – How much the loan is and how much of a down payment you provide will vary the rate you receive.
  - **Character** – Typically only evaluated for business loans, however experienced bankers regard a borrower's character as the utmost important factor in deciding to approve credit. Unfavorable character issues like criminal history, poor credit score without a valid excuse, lack of communication, and other deceptive or shady behavior will make bankers think twice before approving credit.

Auto-loan interest rates are cheaper than credit card interest-rates, because auto lenders have collateral (your car), which it can repossess if you fail to pay back your loan. Credit card debt on the other hand is unsecured, meaning there is no collateral for the credit card company to take in case you fail to pay your bill. Therefore, the credit card company must charge a higher interest rate because they are taking on more risk.

Note, there are consequences to not paying your credit card bill including collection notices, potential lawsuits, and a substantial drop in your credit score which can preclude you from receiving future financing and possibly a new job, as some employers screen candidates credit reports for major negative information.

History on Interest Rates
The foundation of today's interest rates is set by the Federal Reserve's Fed Funds rate, which is the interest rate banks charge other banks to borrow money and is set by the Federal Open Market Committee based in New York.

Large banks and other financial institutions use the Fed Funds rate as a baseline to determine pricing on all other loan products. Any change to the Fed Funds rate has a reverberating effect on all other interest rates. Rates vary from product to product, and borrower to borrower, but it is wise to know how the process starts, because you may be able to time your financing to get an optimal rate. Interest rates have remained low since 2009; however, the Fed Funds rate has been increased from 0.10% in 2008 to 1.75 percent as of early 2018. On paper this may seem like a small increase, but its effects are exponentially larger for the whole financial market including people like us.

The Federal Reserve operates on a dual mandate when deciding how to set interest rates. The dual mandate is price stability and full employment. Price stability means keeping annual inflation at or near 2.00% and full employment is keeping the unemployment at or below 5%.

Common Interest Rates and Benchmarks
- **Fed Funds Rate**
- **LIBOR** – Stands for London Inter Bank Offered Rate and is set daily by 18 of the largest financial institutions. Many commercial and consumer loans are based off this benchmark.
- **Wall Street Journal Prime Rate** – An index rate used by banks to set rates on many commercial and consumer loan products, such as business loans, credit cards, and auto loans.
- **Primary Mortgage Market Survey** – Average mortgage rates from various lenders on a weekly basis. An excellent trend line to look at if you are considering buying a home with a mortgage.

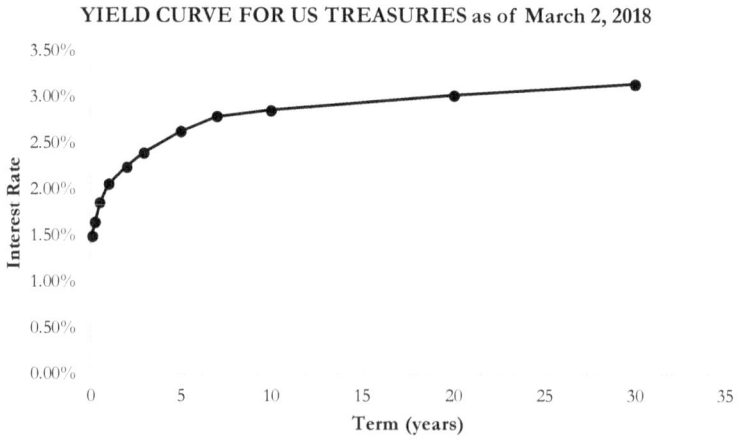

The above chart is the yield curve for U.S. Treasuries, which is U.S. government debt. The U.S. Treasury market is the most liquid and efficient market in the world due to its size and that the debt is backed by the full faith and credit of the U.S. taxpayer.

An upward sloping yield curve generally signals economic growth expectations for the future. A bond's price and yield are inversely related which means, as a bond's price rises, its yield will fall, and vice-versa.

The interest rate (yield) increases as terms get longer because bondholders need to be compensated for the higher risk that comes with longer durations. Risks include inflation and interest rate risk, and the opportunity cost of not investing in a higher yielding asset in the future.

An inverted yield curve (sloping downward) often precedes a recession because investors fearing a recession will buy up longer-term bonds which increase in price and decrease in yield. In this process, investors sell off shorter-term bonds which decrease in price and increase in yield. Hence the downward sloping yield curve. Essentially, investors lose confidence in the economy for the short-term and would rather own long-term bonds they view as safer assets versus owning short-term bonds that suffer from suspected repayment risk due to the expected recession.

Chapter 10: Credit Score

Category	Range
Excellent	750 & Above
Good	700 - 749
Fair	650 - 699
Poor	550 - 649
Bad	550 & Below

A credit score is a number that lenders use to measure an individual's creditworthiness i.e. your ability to repay debt. It is based on your historical debt record from past and current credit cards, mortgages, and other loans. It ranges from 300 being the worst to 850 being the best.

It is important for you to establish a good credit score, so you can be approved for loans on favorable terms. A poor credit score will result in loan declines or subject you to unfavorable terms like higher interest rates and shorter terms, which mean higher monthly payments.

The system (FICO) was created in the early 1980's for financial companies to expand access to credit for its clients. Due to its simple nature FICO scores have become the most popular method lenders use to decision credit for consumers. The three main credit bureaus are Equifax, Experian, and TransUnion. Banks, credit unions, and credit-card companies share their customers' payment history with the credit bureaus that then track the history of repayment and use that information to issue a score on a sliding scale. Based on the model if you have a higher score, you are more likely to pay on time. If you have a lower score, you are likelier to pay late, and possibly default.

Lenders like credit scores because they can be pulled almost instantaneously, which speeds up the approval process compared to the old-fashioned way of writing a time-consuming memo detailing why a consumer should receive a loan. This benefits both borrowers and lenders but does have its downsides. Therefore, it is advantageous for you to know how the scoring system works in order to attain a high score thus receiving more favorable loan terms.

CREDIT SCORE IS DETERMINDED BY:

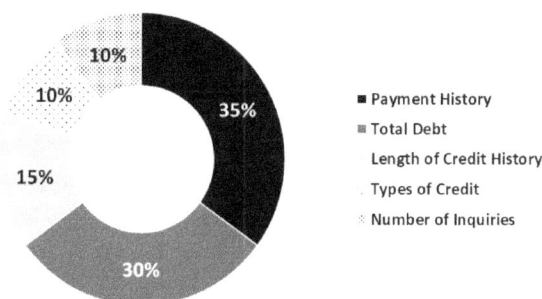

Payment History – 35%
- Do you pay on time? Late payments decrease your score.
- Have you been sent to collections? This will significantly decrease your score.

Total Debt – 30%
- How much debt do you typically have as a percentage of your credit limit? Generally higher debt levels maintained overtime work against you.
- Paying down credit card debt on time increases your score.

Length of Credit History – 15%
- The longer the account is open and in good standing, the higher your score.

Types of Credit – 10%
- Having different types of credit that are in good standing improve your score. Someone with a mortgage, an auto loan, and a credit card all in good standing is regarded as more creditworthy than someone who is in good standing with only a credit card.

Number of Credit Inquiries – 10%
- Your credit score is negatively impacted every time a lender pulls your credit score. Do not be frightened because this is a way lenders hold borrowers accountable for repeatedly seeking credit. Multiple inquiries in a few-day period is considered one inquiry. Multiple pulls over a few weeks and months begin to negatively affect your score, because it means the borrower needs or wants additional money. People who repeatedly need access to credit historically have a higher default rate than those who do not.

Downsides for Borrowers
- **Backward Looking** – It measures only what happened in the past and does not consider anything that happens now or in the future. Hence it is wise to make improvements now so that when you do need a loan you already have a satisfactory score. Changes do not occur overnight.
- **No Score No Loan** – Some borrowers have no credit score because they neither needed credit nor had access to begin to establish credit. Someone in this situation should apply for a credit builder credit card to establish a credit history and build up their score.
- **Not Personal** – Borrowers cannot dispute the credit score with lenders or merchants after the report is run. They must consult the credit bureaus to contest changes putting the loan on hold until the dispute is resolved.

Downsides for Lenders
- **Based Only on Historical Performance** – Just because someone performed well in the past does not mean they will perform well in the future.
- **Not Personal** – Lenders would prefer to know and evaluate the character of its borrowers, however in the interest of time it is not feasible for lenders to evaluate character on all consumer loan applications. Good character is a positive indicator for repayment, yet there are just too many applications, and not enough workers to justify doing this.

Ways to Build and Improve Your Credit Score
- Establish a credit-builder credit card account with a $250-$500 maximum credit limit. Keep it open and in good-standing.
- Pay bills on time or enroll in auto-payments.
- Use credit when appropriate to continue building score. Includes auto-loan, credit cards, mortgage, and other personal loans.
- Monitor your score.
- If in debt trouble, resort to disciplined budgeting, seek advice from a reputable advisor, do your research, and get a second opinion before signing up for debt consolidation.

Chapter 11: Banks v. Credit Unions v. Brokerage Firms

Many people do not have an in-depth understanding of the banking industry. Why should they? Banking terminology can be frustrating, boring, and complex for beginners. Like trying to hit a golf ball for the first few times, picking up banking terms takes a while. But after initial struggles, one can begin to develop a meaningful understanding of the banking landscape, concepts, and vocabulary. Knowing how these concepts work can be presciently used to protect and grow money by capitalizing on opportunities not typically seen by the common person.

Commercial Banks take deposits from businesses and people like us. With those deposits they make loans to creditworthy people and businesses. Their profit is the difference between the interest income and fees they collect from loans and account servicing, over the interest they pay on our deposits, overhead, and taxes.

Credit Unions provide a similar service but to a different clientele. Credit unions are in business to serve its members who are individuals and small businesses that share a commonality like region, employer, or profession. Credit unions are member owned and do not pay taxes which is a competitive advantage they offer its members through pricing. This allows them to often offer more competitive rates than their commercial peers for products like:
- Car loans
- Mortgages
- Home-equity lines of credit

Credit union rates for consumers can be anywhere from 0.10% to 2.00% cheaper than traditional banks.

Why Doesn't Everyone Use a Credit Union?
- Must become a member. Stipulations include employer, organization, or location.
- Geographical footprint is much smaller than commercial banks like Chase, Bank of America, or Wells Fargo.
- Banks typically offer more services and better technology due to their larger size and competitive need.
- Local banks can offer better service.
- Rate difference can be marginal. When looking for a mortgage loan or auto loan, it is best to solicit 3 different rates from multiple lenders to find the best price.

Brokerage Firms specialize in the trading of securities by providing a platform for consumers to buy and sell stocks and bonds with. In addition to all publicly traded securities, brokerage firms usually offer a suite of name-brand mutual funds and ETFs in invest in. Retail investors like you and me will receive discounted trades, or lower commission fees from investing in these funds. Lastly, many retail brokerage firms now offer checking and savings accounts and debit cards directly competing with banks.

Common Accounts
- **Brokerage Account** - used to buy and sell securities with no strings attached.
- **Investment Retirement Account (IRA)** - used for retirement purposes. Can be Roth or traditional.

See Chapters 6, 7, & 8 for more about investing.

Chapter 12: Credit and Debit Cards

In today's digital economy more and more purchases are completed using a credit or a debit card. While cash will always be reserved for certain purchases, it is beneficial to know how these cards work, what the differences are, and ways to optimize your spending to receive rewards.

Credit Cards

A credit card is a loan issued from the credit card company to you. The loan has a maximum amount you can spend, a floating interest rate, and after a certain period if the balance has not been paid off, interest will be due. When your card is used to buy groceries, the credit card company pays the grocery store. You now owe that amount to the credit card company.

The type of loan is a line of credit whereby the lender or credit-card company (American Express, Visa, Master Card) determines your maximum credit amount, and allows you to use that card up to that amount. Once you reach the maximum amount you can no longer use the credit card and need to pay it down to use it again. That is why it is called a credit line, because the line (loan) revolves up and down as you buy things and pay it down.

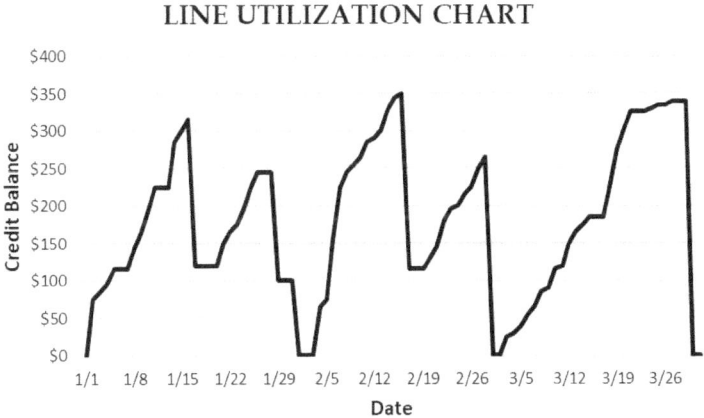

The chart above is a line utilization chart, which illustrates how a credit card is supposed to be used. The credit balance steadily increases as the cardholder pays for items or is charged for monthly subscriptions. Then, as the monthly bill arrives the cardholder pays down the required amount or the full outstanding balance. Credit card companies like to see cardholders revolve the credit line to zero, which demonstrates the capacity to pay back the loan in full on a regular basis. Using your credit card this way will increase your credit score.

How Credit Card Companies Make Money
- Interest paid by customers who do not pay off their credit cards in a timely manner.
- Merchants pay a processing fee (generally 0.5%-2.0% of sales price) to the credit card company for the ability to accept credit cards and the convenience it gives to its customers.

Interest Rates for credit cards are variable so they move in relation to changes on the Fed Funds or Prime rate. As of early 2018, average credit card rates were 16.15%, which is extremely expensive. Credit card companies must charge a higher rate due to higher risk because the loan is unsecured. The credit card company has no collateral and no way to get repaid after default other than selling your loan balance to collections for pennies on the dollar or threatening legal action against the cardholder.

Why Are Credit Cards Good?
- **Convenient** – You can use it multiple times at multiple places without ever having to go to the ATM for cash.
- **Record** – It keeps a record of everything you buy allowing for helpful budget evaluations.
- **Rewards** – You can receive rewards for using your card like cash back, airline miles, or discounts at certain stores.
- **Flexible** – Allows you to buy things you currently do not have the cash for. This is the double-edged sword of credit cards. They provide consumers many benefits but can be abused in the wrong hands.
- **Cash Advance** – You can withdraw money from an ATM with a credit card, but this is strongly discouraged because of its higher fees and rates.

Why Credit Cards Can Be Bad?
- **It Feels Like it is Free** – You swiped your card, and now you have brand new shoes without using available funds. Then, you buy new jeans, and a new jacket thinking you will have time to make money before the bill comes. You get busy the following week and end up not being able to work. The credit card bill dreadfully arrives, and you don't have sufficient funds to make the payment, but still need to buy groceries to live on. Now you are in the hole and must work extra to get out of it.

- **Debt Spiral** – Poor spending choices accelerate the chance to become debt-ridden. It's not surprising that people max out one credit card and transfer the balance to another card thinking that will solve their problem. Yet without making any changes to their spending behavior, this individual will fall right back into punishing debt with their new credit card company. This reflects the beginning of a debt spiral. Individuals in this position need to make better decisions with their spending to slowly climb out of debt. It is unfortunate, but very possible to recover from.
- **Default** – There are serious ramifications to not paying your credit card bill. These include a detrimental hit to your credit score, collection notices, and possible legal actions. Lenders heavily scrutinize applicants with prior defaults or bankruptcies making it more difficult to receive credit approval in the future.

How Are Credit Cards Approved and Limits Determined?
- Credit approval is determined by your credit score. If you have a good score you will be approved for most cards.
- Credit limits are determined by two factors: credit score and stated income.

Providing a false stated income to a financial institution is a crime. Plus, it is prudent that your credit limit fits your needs. There is no point in having a $15,000 credit limit if your annual salary is $35,000.

Rewards
Rewards can be quite attractive if you find a card that fits your lifestyle. Some offer plane tickets, store credit, discounts, and cash back. Select a card that fits your spending and gives you points for things you value.

Debit Cards
A debit card provides the same convenience as a credit card but is linked to your bank account. When you use a debit card the money is deducted from your bank account, and you can only spend up to the amount in your checking account. Furthermore, debit cards allow you to withdraw cash from your bank account at ATMs.

ATM Surcharges
Using your debit card at a different bank than where it was issued will likely have a $2 - $5 surcharge fee to use the ATM. Although frustrating, these fees are standard banking practice. If you frequently withdraw cash, have your accounts at a local bank with nearby branches or ATMs.

Chapter 13: Insurance

Insurance is protection, and when people are protected they live a better life. Insurance comes in many forms with some being essential while others are very specific and not for everyone. The concept and mechanism of insurance broadly remains the same where individuals pay a premium in exchange for a guarantee of compensation in the event of an unfortunate or unpredictable event. When you file a claim, you will have to pay out of pocket up to your deductible then your insurance will kick in. When buying insurance inquire about the coverage types, premiums, and deductible.

Without insurance, people will have to use their emergency savings, liquidate investments, or go into debt to pay for the loss, damage, or injury. Paying a premium now for protection will relieve worry and provide significant gratification when an accident does occur. It will also make you feel pretty wise that you were insured in the first place.

Common Types of Insurance
Health Insurance
- Covers you and or your family in the event of sickness, injury, and regular check-ups. Typically provided through your employer, but some may need to seek out coverage in the private insurance market.
- Be smart about the coverage you select. If you are young and healthy, pick the High Deductible Health Plan, which has lower premiums but covers less. If you have a family and you or your children require regular check-ups, get the PPO, which provides more extensive coverage but at a higher rate.

Renters Insurance
- Covers belongings in a rented area, and liability in case of accidents on rented property. Also may cover living expenses in case of a loss event. Highly recommended and often required by landlords.

Homeowners Insurance
- Covers your property (house) and possessions inside the house from damage. Also covers liability in case of accidents that occur on the property. Required if you have a mortgage. Highly recommended even if your house is paid off.

Life Insurance
- It is wise to have a life insurance policy that fits who you are. Even if you have no dependents, life insurance can ease the financial burden of an awful and unfortunate event. When someone dies, as unfortunate as it is, there are costs associated with that. It pays to have a small life insurance policy that can adequately cover these expenses, instead of having your family cover it. If you are the breadwinner, then life insurance becomes even more important. The higher the face amount of the policy, the higher the premiums will be. Furthermore, the younger and healthier you are, the cheaper the premiums.
    - **Term Life** – Pays a death benefit and only effective for a specified term. Cheaper, and better for younger people.
    - **Whole Life** – Pays a death benefit and accumulates a cash value as time goes on. No term limit if premiums are paid. Typically, better for families, has tax advantages, and is generally more expensive. Do your research before signing a whole life policy.

Auto Insurance
- **Liability Insurance** – All automobiles are required to have this, which insures other drivers for accidents you cause. In theory this protects all drivers on the road, but there will always be a few uninsured motorists on the road causing trouble.
- **Collision** – Insures your vehicle in the event you hit a deer, guardrail, or other fixed object that damages your car.
- **Comprehensive coverage** – Insures your vehicle from being broken into or dented during a hailstorm, or other non-collision event.
- **Uninsured motorist insurance** – Covers your vehicle if an uninsured motorist hits you.
- **Medical payments insurance** – Covers medical payments to you or anyone in your car is hurt in an accident.
- **Personal injury protection** – Like medical payments but it covers a wider array of costs including funeral expense, work-leave, rehabilitation, and replacement services.

Chapter 14: Loans, and How They are Approved

Knowing how to navigate the lending landscape provides valuable benefits for budding entrepreneurs and regular folks alike. Although simple, the old saying "It takes money, to make money" is very true at heart. Any business owner will agree with this concept. Businesses and even people need resources to begin, grow, and sustain themselves just like a seed needs water to germinate, sprout, and grow taller. The amount of money is relative and can be as little as a few bucks to millions of dollars. One has to crawl before they walk and eventually run.

How do loans fit into this picture? Let's start with what the purpose of loan is. A loan is money lent to a business or individual to be used to create or purchase additional value that will generate more value in the future. For commercial purposes, this means the loan proceeds (money) will be used to make more money. Businesses are in business to make money, and they do this by providing value to its customers. Customers would not buy something if they did not think it was worth it. For example, a construction company may use a loan to buy tools and equipment to build a building for a property developer to lease to other businesses who need office space. This is a simple example, but five different parties are being helped by this one loan: the construction company, the developer, the tenant, the tenant's customers, and the bank.

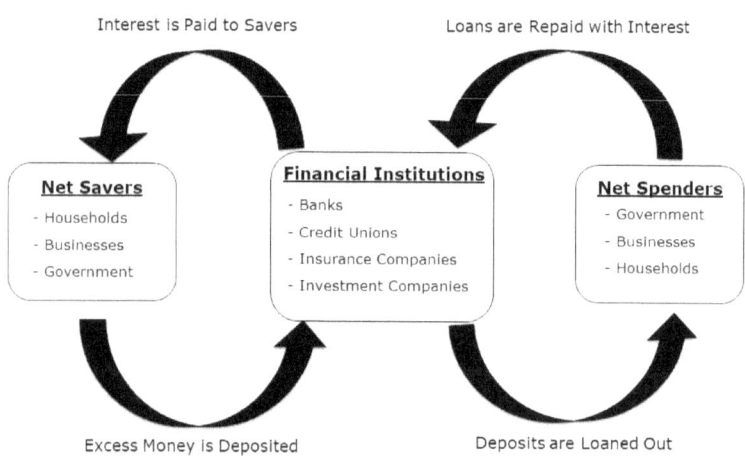

Banks and other financial institutions facilitate financial intermediation, which is matching savers with borrowers. The bank will lend out people's deposits to businesses that will use the money for more productive uses. In turn, the business pays back the loan plus interest. The bank then pays interest to depositors for being able to loan that money out in the first place.

Commercial loans will vary in size, type, and mechanics, but the underwriting concept remain the same. Underwriting is where lenders assess the purpose of the loan, risks of default, and creditworthiness of the borrower. This allows a lender to make an informed credit decision.

The levels of risk lenders assume influence the interest rate of the loan. Higher risk loans require higher rates of interest because lenders need to be compensated for a higher probability of not being repaid. Banks are stewards of people's money therefore it is vital for them to make sound credit decisions. Bankers are risk managers, and in business to both protect depositors' money and earn a return sufficient to sustain operations.

Banks help support the community. They assist businesses by providing needed capital to expand operations, construct new buildings, and hire more workers.

Types of Commercial Loans
- **Line of Credit** – Lines of credit are used to finance timing differences of a company's cash flows (revenues and expenses) also called working capital. The mechanics are like a credit card.
- **Term Loan** – Just like an auto loan. A term loan is a set amount of money to be repaid over a set period of time. Term loans are used for start-up expenses, vehicles, equipment, debt consolidation, tenant finish-out, dividends, and more.
- **Real Estate Loan** – Same mechanics as a term loan however used to purchase real property like a building or land.
- **Construction Draw Loan** – Line of credit, which is only allowed to be drawn upon to pay for construction costs of real property. The bank disburses loan proceeds as construction costs are incurred. It would be imprudent for a bank to give the developer all the money upfront when it may take months or years to complete the building.

Bankers Underwrite Loans Using the 5 C's of Credit

1. **Capital** – Also called the down payment. Borrowers who are more willing to put their own money into the project are looked at more favorably because they have skin in the game. For example, a bank would laugh at providing 100% financing to a developer, because the bank would be taking all the risk.
2. **Capacity** – This is cash flow and repayment. How is the loan going to repaid? Without a repayment source, bankers will never grant credit.
3. **Conditions** – Loans are written in a legal contract enforceable by the rule of law requiring borrowers and lenders to abide by a set of ground rules. These conditions require or restrict the borrower and lender from doing certain things, stipulates rules in the event of contingencies, reduces risk, and works to ensure repayment.
4. **Collateral** – Assets that are pledged to the loan. In the event of default, banks will take the collateral to pay back the loan. Collateral values vary depending on the loan and at times can be unsecured.
5. **Character** – The most important factor in deciding credit approval. This is the borrower's credit history and reputation. A person or business with a poor reputation for repaying their debts will have a difficult time receiving credit. On the contrary an entrepreneur who is committed and level headed will fare much better at receiving credit approval so long as the loan request is logical and feasible.

SBA Loans

Small Business Association is a federal agency created to help small businesses receive credit to grow their business. SBA loans are less restrictive and more accessible to newer companies without much credit history because the SBA will guarantee a portion of the loan.
Commercial banks offer these loans by working together with the SBA.

Good Candidates for SBA Loans

- Startup Businesses
- Companies with excessive leverage
- Companies with cash flow constraints that need more favorable debt terms

SBA 7(a) Business Loan Program

The 7(a) loan is the SBA's primary loan product for small businesses. The bank will agree to provide a loan to the borrower contingent upon the SBA providing a guarantee from 50% to 85% of the loan amount. This means that if the loan defaults, the SBA is on the hook for whatever percentage it guaranteed after all collateral is liquidated. Although the SBA guaranty is not used by the bank to replace collateral, it does help the bank extend more flexible loan terms to the borrower.

- Max Loan amount: $5,000,000
- Term: between 2 years and 25 years
- Minimum Down Payment: 10% - 25% of total project
- Uses: Start-up costs, expansion, equipment purchases, working capital, inventory, debt refinance, change of ownership, or business-occupied real-estate purchases.

SBA 504 or Certified Development Company Loan

The loan is split into two, a 50% percent portion from the bank, and 40% portion from the local Certified Development Company (CDC). A CDC is state-chartered private company certified by the SBA to assist small businesses in securing financing.

- Max Loan amount: $5,000,000
- Term: between 2 years and 25 years
- Minimum Down Payment: 10% - 20% of total project
- Uses: Finance commercial real estate, construction, tenant improvements, or equipment.

Chapter 15: Developing A Business Plan

Most people will never start or own their own business. Let's face it there are few entrepreneurs among us. Some try, but many fizzle out. The ones who persist or come up with a novel idea reap the rewards through ingenuity, determination, and good fortune.

The others in between may not win big, or even scratch the surface of popular success, but would never have known if they hadn't tried in the first place. This is the way our economy works. The ones who provide the best value get rewarded, while the others do not.

Think of a market. You are free to roam, look, and buy. But you don't have to buy if you don't agree with the price. If you cannot find a better price, but believe you can provide it cheaper or better, than that is a market opportunity for you to profit from. You can now be the entrepreneur, the business owner, the risk-taker, and profit seeker. All you have to do is start. But how? Welcome to the business plan.

Business Plan Components

1. **Company Description**
   - What will the company provide?

2. **Industry Overview**
   - Is there a need for your product or service?
   - How is the market for your product of service changing?

3. **Business Strategy**
   - What will you focus on so your product sells?
   - How will you differentiate from the competition?

4. **Competitive Landscape**
   - Is another business already providing this product or service?
   - Is there room for you to enter and take market share?

5. **Operating Plan**
   - How will you execute your business so that your product or service can get to market?

6. **Financial Summary**
    - How much capital do you need to start and sustain operations for the short and long-term?
    - What is your price, and targeted profit margins?
    - Will you be taking on debt or investor money that needs to be repaid?

7. **Management/Team**
    - Who owns the company?
    - Who will manage and operate the company?
    - What is their experience and how will it benefit the company?

A simple business plan is consistently better than a complex one. Each component needs only a couple logical sentences. The reason is, many start-ups face unexpected issues and unforeseen events once they begin. No person or business can predict the future with certainty. Therefore, keep your business plan simple, and leave the door open for contingency planning. It is a cliché but 'expect the unexpected' and be willing to deviate from the plan for the better of the business. The business plan is just a data plan to start. The plan must change as necessary directs or opportunity offers.

Although many of us will never need to write a business plan, it is beneficial to know its contents and purpose. We will all work for an organization that is striving to provide value to someone or something. Knowing what, why, and how will make you a better asset to your team.

Chapter 16: Buying a Vehicle

Buying an automobile is something most people will have to do multiple times in their lifetime. Besides a house, buying an automobile is likely the next most expensive purchase they will make. A car is a big-ticket item, and it is wise to think about what you are buying, and why you are buying it just as much as how much to spend.

Before we get into the numbers, it is important to know first what type of car you want and why. This is just as important as the cost because people use their automobiles daily, and it is wise to get something that fits who you are and is practical for your lifestyle. A single person should not be getting a van or large SUV unless they intend to haul people around often. Nor should a construction worker get a Prius knowing full well that they regularly have to haul materials to job sites.

Story – This reminds me of a guy I knew from Llano, Texas. His name was Dustin, was recently married and looking to purchase a new vehicle to replace his old beat up pickup truck. During our talk, he mentioned that he and his wife were looking at fuel-efficient cars like the Toyota Prius to save money on his 30-minute daily commute to work. After working with Dustin for a couple years, I got to know him well. He was a guy that wore cowboy boots with his suit. There was no way I could see Dustin being happy in a Prius no matter how much money he was saving. Instantly, I told him, "Dustin, you are a truck guy. Get a truck. This is a decision that will stick with you for a long time." The following week, with a wide grin Dustin popped into my office saying, "I did it. I got a new truck!" He ended up getting a Toyota Tacoma, a mid-sized truck with decent fuel economy. He even used the truck to haul things that weekend. It was a win-win. Dustin got the vehicle he enjoys that fits his lifestyle, and one that won't guzzle down his wallet with gas expense.

Point being is to pick a type of vehicle that is practical for you, something you can enjoy, because on average it will be with you for the next 5-7 years.

Knowing Your Budget
Now let's get to the financial side of buying a car. First thing you need is a ballpark estimate of what you want to spend. Ballparking your budget is better than setting a strict amount, because sometimes you can hamstring yourself into not getting what you really want, because of a strict budget and end up compromising with something that is just okay in your mind.

Of course, the final cost is critical so do not buy more than you can afford or maintain just to keep up with appearances.

Arrange Financing Before Going to the Dealer
It is best to solicit an auto loan request from your local bank or credit union before going to the dealer. This offers leverage and the ability to find out what you qualify for. The credit union or bank will run your credit and provide you with a blank check up to an amount you qualify for. This check pre-qualifies you to buy any automobile on the lot up to that amount and is your leverage to negotiate a more favorable price from the dealer. Remember the interest rate that the credit union or bank provides, because it is possible, but not often that the dealer will be able to match or beat it.

Negotiation
After you have found the vehicle that you want and that is in your price range, it is time to negotiate. Keep in mind dealers typically do not reduce the price for vehicles that are hot and in-demand, because they know someone will come in and purchase it at market value. So, haggle wisely, and know the Kelly Blue Book values before you walk on the lot. Let the salesperson know that you are pre-qualified and want to buy. Ask for a price 10% to 20% below sticker value and see what they come back with. It is important to start lower, because as the buyer, you want the lowest price, and vice-versa for the dealer.

After a couple turns, you and the dealer will get closer to the middle. If you are not satisfied by their best offer find out if they can better the price if you finance with the dealer. Dealers earn additional revenue for referring buyers to the manufacturers financing subsidiary. They may even reduce the price; however what interest rate you receive affects the overall total cost of the automobile.

Crunch the Numbers
Do the math to calculate your total interest expense over the life of both loans. Make sure to include any additional discount the dealer gives you provided that you finance with them. Choose the cheapest option.

Lastly, the term of the loan dictates the interest rate. The longer the term, the higher your interest rate will be, and the lower payment you will have. Pick a term that fits in your budget. If you can afford the shorter-term loan with a higher payment without straining your budget, then it is wise to pick the shorter term. Plus, with this option you will pay less in interest, and will pay off the loan sooner.

Benefits of Buying versus Leasing
- Build equity (ownership) of your car with each payment.
- The equity you build is valuable when you decide to sell or trade-in.
- No mileage restrictions.

Benefits of Leasing
- You can afford a more expensive automobile because you are only paying for the depreciation of the vehicle. Depreciation is the decrease in value as the automobile ages and is utilized.
- The monthly payments are usually cheaper however you build no equity.

Drawbacks of Leasing
- There are strict mileage restrictions. Fees are assessed if you go over this limit.
- Vehicle maintenance is a must. If you do not properly maintain and document the maintenance, penalty fees will be due at lease termination.

Recommendation
In the long-run you are better off financially buying, because of the equity you build. Properly service your vehicle, and it will have trade-in value when it's time to buy a new car again.

Story – Never agree to allow someone to make payments on an auto-loan that is in your name. Here is a story about my friend Scott, who met a lady, and began dating shortly after. Five months into the relationship, all was well but this fine lady needed an automobile. She found the perfect Jeep Wrangler Sport that all the cool kids had and needed this vehicle. But she had no credit, because she never established a credit history and relied on her parents. She had been earning enough to satisfy the loan payments but could not qualify for a loan. So lovestruck Scott stepped up to the plate and put the loan in his name. Long story short, the couple split up, and Scott is now stuck paying for two car loans, his and his ex-girlfriends, and he doesn't even have possession of the new Jeep. He had to verbally fight with his ex to get the car back and unceremoniously sold it back to the dealer for a small loss, but happy to have concluded the affair. Ultimately Scott learned a good lesson, so heed his mistake so you don't learn the hard way.

Chapter 17: Buying a House

Buying a house is likely the single largest purchase one will make in their lifetime. It is critically important to understand the process, prepare wisely, and engage aggressively to make the best possible decision. Buying a home is emotional, because it is a decision with long term ramifications with countless things to consider like price, size, location, school district, and which real estate agent to use. Making these decisions without much thought and reflection will lead to regret, headache, and quite possibly financial loss. Asking questions and learning the process on the front-end will make your home buying experience much less stressful which lends itself to a more successful outcome. Fortunately, this section will provide you with the basics so you can confidently buy your first home.

Is Home Ownership Right for You?
First thing is to find out if home ownership is right for you. Even though home ownership is typically cheaper in the long run, not all people should buy a home. People should continue renting if they expect to move within 3 years.

Renting Benefits
- Convenience and flexibility.
- Liquidity advantages – Do not need to plunk down a large down payment.
- Diversification – By renting you can use your capital for investments other than real estate. In many times instances a person's home becomes their largest asset making their net worth susceptible to market downturns.
- Renting can be cheaper, sometimes.

Buying Advantages
- Should be less expensive
- Great way to build wealth
- Not susceptible to rising rental prices. Think inflation
- Build equity in home, which can appreciate, and can be used to borrow against with a HELOC.
- Don't have to deal with landlords.
- Can get a mortgage with only 3% to 5% down-payment

When deciding to buy a home, think about the future cost of renting versus owning. If you are to stay in the same place for a while, it is typically better to buy, because of the equity you build and the fixed housing cost you will pay. Taxes and insurance will vary slightly, but your housing costs will be relatively fixed compared with rent, which fluctuates annually.

If buying is right for you, then it is necessary to get a clear picture of your financials to find out what you can afford. The beauty of modern finance is that you can buy a $200,000 house without actually having all that the money right now. However, a down payment is required and the standard amount is usually 20%. Therefore, if you want that $200,000 house, then having $40,000 for the down payment will make the mortgage process easier and cheaper.

Loan to Value (LTV) is a term used to assess the current state of the loan relative to the value of the collateral, which is the house. At closing, if your home's LTV is 80% then you made a 20% down payment. The value at closing is fair market value, which is what you and the seller both agreed was a fair price. In 2009 during the mortgage crisis, many homeowners became underwater on their mortgage, because the outstanding mortgage balance exceeded the fair market value of the house. This results in a LTV greater than 100%.

If you are not able to put 20% down, most lenders will require private mortgage insurance (PMI). This is an additional required monthly fee insuring the lender if you default. Once your LTV reaches 80%, PMI will no longer be required. Ask your mortgage lender about first time homebuyer programs that may help reduce the overall cost.

The down payment acts as a cushion for the lender in case the borrower defaults and real estate prices fall. They do not want to repossess a house in which its fair market value is worth less than the outstanding mortgage balance, because they will lose money selling it in foreclosure. Remember, mortgage lenders are in the business of providing loans to homebuyers, not the buying and selling of real estate.

It is your responsibility to find out what you can afford. Mortgage lenders will only tell you what you can qualify for. Mortgage applicants often qualify for loans that exceed the amount they can afford, because mortgage lenders do not take into account their full lifestyle budget.

Lenders require a debt to income of no more than 45%. This means that your total monthly debt including the proposed mortgage payment, taxes, and insurance cannot be greater than 45% of your total monthly income. See calculation on next page.

monthly
Mortgage Payment (P&I)
+ Property Taxes
+ Insurance
+ Student Debt
+ Auto Loan
+ Other Debt Payments
= Total Monthly Debt

$$\frac{\text{Monthly Debt}}{\text{Monthly Gross Income}} = 45\%$$

*DTI can be no more than 45%

Remember that the Debt to Income (DTI) calculation ignores groceries, utilities, retirement savings, housing maintenance costs, and other obligations. Rule of thumb on average property owners spend about 1% of the purchase price on maintenance each year.

Fixed v. Adjustable Rate Mortgages
Mortgages come in two types of rates: fixed and adjustable. Fixed rates stay the same throughout the life of the loan. That means one will have the same mortgage payment every month until the mortgage is paid off. Fixed rates make budgeting and planning much easier.

Conversely, adjustable rate mortgages (ARM) adjust at certain times specified in the mortgage contract. What makes ARMs attractive is that they usually start with a lower interest rate compared to its fixed counterpart thereby making it easier to qualify. A common ARM is a 3/1, which has a fixed rate for the first 3 years of the mortgage, then a variable rate for the remaining 27 years of the mortgage. The variable rate is governed by a spread (margin) on a published index (benchmark) which is usually a specific treasury yield or the Wall Street Journal prime rate. Each year after the 3rd year, the rate will adjust according to its spread and index. Therefore, if rates go down, owners with ARM's will benefit, however if rates rise, then owners with ARM's will have a higher payment. ARM's also come in 1 year, 5 year, 7 year and 10 year hybrid formats.

Reasons for an Adjustable Rate Mortgage
- One has the capacity to buy the house in full with cash, but prefers to finance with an ARM to take advantage of the more attractive initial lower rate. This individual has the luxury to take the chance that future rates will decrease making his ARM even more attractive. The gamble is worth it because if rates rise too much for his liking he can pay off the balance in full.
- The owner expects to live in the house for only a few years. By matching the fixed rate portion of the ARM to the time period

he expects to live in the house will allow the homebuyer to realize the lower initial rate offered on the ARM. This is a sound strategy to save money, but it is not risk-free. Exposure to the real estate market at time of sale, interest rate swings, and plans not evolving as expected are risks that need to be considered.

For most people I recommend a fixed rate mortgage because it makes planning and budgeting easier. Yet for certain situations and individuals ARM's are the better deal. Just know trying to time the market exactly or predicting what rates will be in the future is a losing persons game.

15 Year Term v. 30 Year Term

Mortgage terms typically come in 15 years and 30 years. The 30 year term will have a higher interest rate than the 15 year term, because lenders need to be compensated for the increased risk of default with longer term loans. With that being said the 30 year term provides a lower payment, because one will be paying twice as long compared to the 15 year term. However, one will pay much more in total interest over the life of the loan on the 30 year mortgage. Have your mortgage broker break out the total interest costs over the life of both loans so you can visually see the difference. See example below.

Interest Rate Cost Difference Between 15 & 30 Year Term For a $150,000 Mortgage at 4.45%

	15 year	30 year
Monthly Payment	$ 1,144	$ 756
Total Interest Paid	$ 55,859	$ 122,008
Total Amount Paid	$ 205,859	$ 272,008

Pick a term that you can conservatively pay back. Remember, unless you have a mortgage with a prepayment penalty you can always pay back the 30 year mortgage quicker if you want. However, there is no grace if you sign up for the 15 year term and cannot come up with the monthly payment.

I highly advise against getting a mortgage with a prepayment penalty. These are clauses in the contract that penalize you with fees if you pay off the mortgage quicker than the agreed upon term. The fee amount is usually the lost interest on the loan, which the mortgage lender wants, because it is their source of revenue. Furthermore, having a prepayment penalty complicates the sales process if you wish to sell your house with an outstanding balance on the mortgage.

Find a Mortgage Lender That Is:
- Well known in the local community
- Straight forward and detailed
- Knowledgeable about the market and interest rate environment
- Open to discuss the competition and offer a value proposition

Buying the Right House for the Right Price

This is where finding the right real estate agent is worth their weight in gold to you. A good real estate agent will take the time to understand what you want, find listings suitable to your criteria, and will negotiate on your behalf to get you the best deal. To find a good agent, ask trusted professionals and friends for referrals, and make sure to interview the agent to see if you will have a good working relationship.

Find a Real Estate Agent Who:
- Will educate you on the market providing comparable sales
- Is passionate about their job
- Has time to answer your questions
- Is professional about the business
- Is prompt and transparent
- Is educated and credentialed with proper designations

The seller typically pays the real estate commission, which averages between 4% to 7% of the sales price. This amount will be split between the buyer's agent and the seller's agent. Furthermore, if the agent is not also a broker, then the brokerage firm involved will take a cut.

Closing

Always make your offer subject to review and approval of all inspection reports. Due diligence on the structural condition of the house is paramount to reduce the risk of having to pay for costly repairs.

Homebuying Tips
1. Assemble a good team (real estate agent, mortgage lender, inspector, escrow officer, etc.) They will provide valuable advice and help you through the process.
    - Get to know them personally. If you involve yourself and take initiative, they will know you are committed and will work harder for you.
2. Know the inherent conflicts of interest. Agents, lenders, and everyone else only get paid if you buy. Before reaching out to an agent, first know if buying is right for you.
3. Shop mortgage lenders to find best rate and structure. Sometimes, the lowest rate is not the cheapest due to more points up front, which is the additional fees paid to lender. I recommend soliciting 3 mortgage lenders and comparing each offer.
4. Don't buy the most expensive house on the street. Buy a cheaper one, because the more expensive houses nearby will pull up the other homes value.
5. Before you buy the house, think about selling it down the road. Will there be trouble selling it due to odd features?
6. Negotiate the fees and speak up if something doesn't seem right.

Chapter 18: Wealth

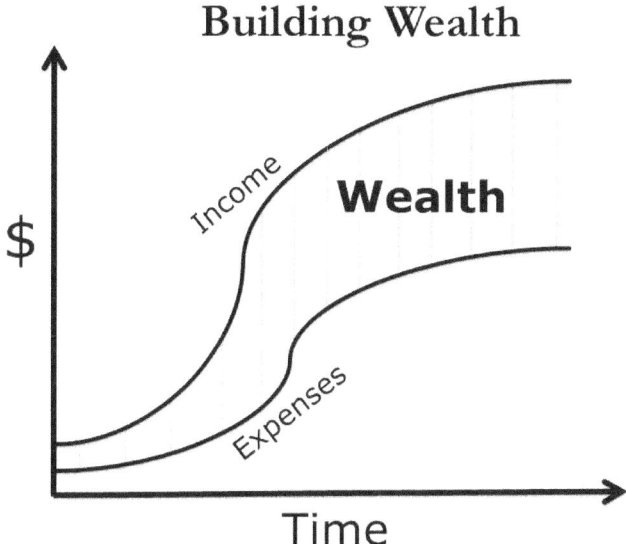

There is a universal law for income, which is there is no ceiling to how much money one can make. Let me reiterate that point one more time, there is no limit to how much money a person can make. Naysayers may protest arguing they do not have the time or ability, yet those are just excuses. If you want to have more money, you must find ways to earn more money. This can take many forms including taking on a part-time job, selling baked goods or widgets at a local farmers market, purchasing a rental property, making more sales at work, or earning a promotion through hard work.

On the flipside, there is also a universal law regarding expenses, which is there will always be a floor to how little one can reduce expenses. Specifically, one will always have living experiences therefore there is a hard limit to how much one can save by spending less. This does not imply that you should not reduce expenses where appropriate. Sound budgeting always remain strongly encouraged. The point of the laws is to illustrate there are more ways to earn more money than there are ways to save more money.

Overtime as the proportion of income exceeds that of expenses, these savings if used correctly will build wealth, which include investments, real estate, personal property, and other assets.

Chapter 19: Becoming Rich

Being rich is all about how you define it. Without deciding what rich is for yourself, you will be stuck with accepting and believing how popular culture defines rich to be, which is having a huge house, flying private, driving expensive cars, taking exotic vacations, or wearing only the finest clothes. These are the typical traits associated with famous people you see on TV. However, rich people come in many forms and not all act or spend the way TV may depict. There are ultrawealthy billionaires, of which there are very few, well-to-do millionaires, and ordinary people. You might never know it, but the modest neighbor living across the street from you may have accumulated ample wealth to never have to worry about money again. Although the neighbor has exorbitantly less money than a billionaire, he or she can still be considered rich because they have enough money to happily cover their family's needs and wants, and that is all that matters to them.

In America, we grow up aspiring to be better than how we started. This ethos comes from the immigrants who first came here. They experienced extreme hardship in their native lands, voyaged to America for a better future, and succeeded in constructing the most free and dominant country in the world. Every American who aspires for something is free to pursue it, and that collective spirit we share is what makes our country so amazing. If you work hard for something, you can achieve it. Whether that be financial wealth or something else is up to you.

Capitalism breeds competition making us smarter and stronger, ultimately producing better goods and services. It is this self-organizing system that is the platform for getting better and wanting more. If you want more, you must provide more which requires more responsibility or ingenuity. People who choose to take on these difficult challenges whether at work or through entrepreneurial ventures will be rewarded for their success with monetary benefits. This is capitalism.

Follow Your Intuition
If you desire to be rich, follow your intuition and you will be rewarded with not only money but pride, accomplishment, and meaning. Be prepared to make sacrifices, for if it were easy everyone would do it. The keyword is intuition, which is the power in your mind that knows right from wrong. Trusting your intuition will lead you to success. Look inside yourself to find out what you are good at, which is probably what you enjoy doing. Someone that likes people, parties, and music may make a good DJ, party planner, or network organizer. One who enjoys art may

make a good photographer, Instagram curator, or graphic designer. Or one who enjoys beer may make a good brewer, beer reviewer, or hops grower. Keep in mind that the amount of money you earn is in direct relation to the value you provide and the amount of people you provide that to.

Finding Your Intuition
Sometimes to learn more about yourself, you need to get out of your current environment and surround yourself in different scenery. Take a few hours or days to yourself and reflect on the things you like and why. Oftentimes, if we are stuck doing the same things over and over again, our mind goes on autopilot, and we become like a drone unable to think differently. Changing the scenery frees us from our normal day-to-day life allowing new thoughts to pour in. This is the ideal time to experiment with your thoughts to learn more about yourself.

Being Rich and Happy
Good! This is a worthwhile goal and absolutely possible. First of all being happy is a state of mind, and only you can decide that. Nothing else matters. Not your job, not your spouse, not your friends, not your family. Only you can choose to be happy by choosing what is important to you and taking action to achieve or keep what is important.

Being rich is also a state of mind. One can earn a low wage loving what they do, and feel rich, because the compensation allows them to provide for themselves and continue doing what they love. With that said this person still needs to practice sound budgeting, establish emergency savings, and contribute to their retirement account.

Financial Goals
It is important to have financial goals, but not being happy until you reach that certain milestone is a fool's game. Set a realistic goal first. Make it hard, but achievable. Then, be diligent about realizing that goal by committing to it and by monitoring it to see where you succeed and where you fall short. Continue to focus on your goal, and once you have accomplished it, set another one!

Money Rich
If you want to make millions, or hundreds of thousands of dollars, then you must work hard and take risk. That means educating yourself to become a highly sought after professional or create something that makes people's lives better. These are calculated risks paying off only if you are providing something of extreme value.

What if I Don't Like My High Paying Job, But the Jobs I Would Enjoy Don't Pay Nearly Enough?

This is an example of being in a situation that's causing your values to conflict. One would need to reconcile their values by deciding what is more important to them: money or happiness. Maybe, happiness is derived from the money that provides for his or her family. Someone in this position is making a sacrifice to ensure their family's welfare, because they value their family more than their work. This can be viewed as honorable. This individual may want to stay in their job but find ways to devote more time to his or her vocation.

Occupation v. Vocation

Remember that your occupation, what you do for an income does not have to be your vocation, which is your calling. Your occupation provides the means for you and your family to live a financially secure life. But between work, you can focus your energy on your vocation which is something that truly matters to you in a different way, like volunteering, playing music, watching movies, decorating, writing, carpentry, riding motorcycles, playing videogames, golfing, socializing, fishing, gardening, painting, cooking, traveling, studying history, and so much more. Kudos to you if your vocation can also provide a financial benefit.

It is rare, but most people's occupation is not their vocation. Be cognizant of this, and work to find a balance between the two, because when your occupation gets stressful, you will need your vocation to lean on.

Until Next Time…

- Take time to understand how each one of your financial decisions will affect your life, no matter how small or immaterial they may seem.

- Practice good habits. Results only come through disciplined practice, commitment, and patience.

- Don't be afraid of risk. Calculate it and make a decision.

- Pursue what is meaningful to you, whether that is through your vocation and or occupation.

- Never stop learning. It is a lifelong process.

- Setbacks will occur. Keep picking yourself up and working towards your goal.

- Believe in yourself.

About the Author

Dan Gasapo worked as an analyst for a commercial bank in Austin, Texas underwriting loans for small and medium sized businesses and learned invaluable lessons from his co-workers and clients. Gasapo is a graduate of St. Bonaventure University and resides in New York.

Available on **Amazon.com**

Tweet **@ExtremeMoney2**

Templates available at **https://goo.gl/BBVzbo**

www.ingramcontent.com/pod-product-compliance
Lightning Source LLC
Chambersburg PA
CBHW070211230526
45471CB00002B/923